CAPRI

BONECHI

A picturesque view of Capri as seen from the peninsula of Sorrento.

INTRODUCTION

In the everchanging and vast panorama of the minor islands of Italy, Capri holds a position of absolute priviledge. If on the one hand every island has well-defined characteristics and special particularities which help to give a tourist image, on the other hand the very mention of Capri — evokes an inextricable mixture of sensations which exalt the dimensions of a Mediterranean island par excellence.

Capri is essentially a fairy tale, a dream lost in the extra-ordinary azure of an incredible sea, in the boundless panoramas which embrace other precious tesserae of that wonderful mosaic which is the Neapolitan and Salerno coast, between Capo Miseno and Amalfi.

Everything which can be perceived by the senses finds its greatest elevation on this island; from the light, sublime complement and refined facets of colour which allow one to read, as in an open book, the endless wonders of the place; from the perfume of the flowers which constitute another jewel of the island and the vegetation which is a mixture of Mediterranean aspects and more precisely tropical ones: from the strong salt-laden breezes of a sea which is the very life of the island; from the disturbing voice of silence, broken only by the piercing cry of the seagulls and the breaking of the waves on the steep and precipitous rocks; from the possibility of touching with one's own hands the ancient traces of an illustrious and fascinating history, together with numerous remains of a past which represents the most authentic cultural metrix of the place; from the rough, yet sublime taste of the re-fined cuisine of Capri, to the rich taste of its noble wines produced on rough but generous land.

GEOGRAPHICAL PROFILE

The island which is frequently linked to the mainland (Naples and Sorrento) by boats and hovercraft is only 5 kms from Punta Campanella, which represents the furthermost point of the Sorrento peninsular. Its polulation (12.500 approx.) is spread out over the two Comunes of Capri and Anacapri. The total surface area is around 11 square kms and measures approximately 6 kms in length and at its widest point measures around 3 kms. The circumference of its coasts measures 17 kms.

In the most remote geolological era Capri was definitely part of the morphological and structural unity of the Sorrent peninsular, from which it was later separated due to the major techtonic and orogenetic upheavals. Unlike the Flegree islands which are situated in front of the Campi Flegree in the upper portion of the wide Neapolitan gulf, Capri does not have vulcanic origins.

The island is set in front of the Sorrento peninsular, from which it is separated by a narrow strait of water called Bocca Piccola. The geological structure of Capri is prevalently calcarea with the presence of tuff and pozzuolana transported by the winds during the paroxysmal vulcanic eruptions of Campi Flegree and Vesuvius. The coasts which are high and rocky offer a large number of grottoes and are surrounded by rocks which rise out of the water, such as the famous Faraglioni. The highest mountains are Mount Solaro (589 m) the Mount St. Maria (499 m) and Mount Tiberius (335 m).

Capri has very few rivers (although there are a few small transitory streams in the westernmost area) and because of the complete lack of springs a plant for extracting salt from sea water has recently been installed so as to provide the drinking water necessary for the population and for the numerous tourists.

The flora of Capri has characteristcs which are similar to that of the Sorrento peninsular and has a decidedly Mediterranean aspect including the presence of well over 850 species and 133 varieties. The fauna of the island consists mainly of seagulls even though rare animals such as the sea-cow (Monachus monachus) are to be found although unfortunately they are becoming extinct. Also to be found is the singular *Lacerta coerulea faraglionensis* commonly known as the blue lizard.

The characteristics of the climate of Capri are typical of a Mediterranean island and therefore result in numerous mild days throughout the year. Even in summer the temperatures are generally under 30° and this is thanks to the moderate yet constant sea breezes which, as well as having a thermo-regulator function, keep the island free from damp sea mists, exalting the spectacular island scenery accentuated by an intensely clear blue sky. In winter the temperatures are, on the whole, quite pleasant, with a complete absence of frost.

The economic structure of Capri is largely based on tourism which, in the last decades, has enjoyed a boom. Probably Capri's reputation as a tourist Mecca dates back to the last century when it was discovered by the Swedish writer and doctor Axel Munthe and was visited by such illustrious names as Ferdinand Gregorovius, Alexandre Dumas, August von Platen-Hallermünde and others. In more recent times Maxim Gorki, Curzio Malaparte and Ada Negri consolidated and perpetuated the tradition of the island as a paradise for meditation and inspiration. A refined first-class hotel structure, a high level of recreational structures and its fame as a seaside resort all contribute in making Capri a Mecca of international tourism. Another important aspect of the island's economy is the fishing industry and the handicraft industry — which produces beautiful ceramics and majolica, coral jewelry, hand-made baskets and large whicker baskets, and espadrilles — important crops (vines and olive groves), citrus fruits, together with other cottage industries (textiles and woodwork).

HISTORY

Of the many versions given for the origin of the placename — *Caprea* according to Strabone, to indicate the harsh conformation of its rocky soil, or *Capraim* which comes from a semitic expression which means "two villages" — *Capreae* is without doubt the more convincing because it would refer as Varone ascertaines, to the considerable presence of wild boars on the island (*Caprios* according to Greek spelling). The fact that Capri was a Greek colony is now certain even if it is believed that it was populated as far back as the palaeolithic age, during the period of major vulcanic activity in the Flegrea regions, when the island formed part of the mainland. This latter ascertion is backed by the extraordinary archeological discoveries which date back to Roman times, when, during the building of monumental villas, the bones of prehistoric animals and stone weapons were found. At the beginning of this century, during excavation work for the foundations of the Quisisana Hotel other prehistoric weapons and the bones of animals such as the *Rhinoceros Merckii*, the *Ursus spelaeus* and the *Elephas primigenius* were found. If the Greek prescence on Capri can be proved by the numerous greek epigraphs and by the existence, during the Roman Imperial Age of a greek term used to describe the appointing of municipal magistrates (*agoranómi*), the presence of the Phoenicians who seem to have established the commercial landing places on the island has yet to be proved. The Roman "discovery" of Capri dates back to 29 A.D. when Augustus landed here on his way back to Rome after the Eastern campangs. Having fallen in love with the island, he took it from the Neapolitans, giving them Ischia in return. His presence marks a transformation in the juridicial and administrative aspects of the island, which from this date would undergo radical changes due to the building work done on the island such as the construction of sumptuous villas and splendid residences.

After the death of Augustus (14 A.D.) his successor Tiberius, made Capri his "golden exile", choosing the is-

land as his home for the last decade of his life. The chronicles of Tacito and Svetonio give a dark and gloomy portrait of Tiberius underlining the most perverse and evil aspects of his character, without paying hommage to the notable qualities of the man, which a more objective and indirect historiographical judgement would surely give. His death (37 A.D.) which took place near the Villa of Lucullo at Miseo, whilst he was trying to reach his beloved island, marked the beginning of the decline of Capri together with the changing attitude of the Romans towards the island, who, apart from a few exceptions, would, from this point onwards, use it as an exile for people who created trouble in the capital.

Such was the destiny of Lucilla and Crispina, respectively the sister and the mother of the Emperor Commodo (182 A.D.).

At the fall of the Roman Empire Capri was controlled by the abbots of Montecasino and by Neapolitans, and was subjected to frequent pirate raids especially those of the Saracens. Then it was controlled by the Longobards who were followed by the Normans and then the island passed from one domination to another including the Aragonesi, Angioini, and the raids of the Turkish pirates Khair ad-Din (*Barbarossa*) and Dragut. For a long time it came under Spanish administration and suffered a great plague (18th century), and then finally it was governed by the Borbons. It was contended by the French and English at the time of the Napoleonic Wars, after which it was ruled once more by the Borbons of Naples before its annexation to the newly formed Kingdom of Italy thereby establishing the characteristics which it now maintains as one of the obligatory stages of the international tourism.

A view of the majestic Faraglioni.

*Marina Grande and its port, at the foot of
Mount Solaro.*

MARINA GRANDE

It is difficult for a person who does not know Capri to imagine the emotions and the surprise of the tourist or traveller who sets foot on this enchanted island for the first time. Marina Grande, as is quite clear from its name, is the main port and the most frequented landing place of the island as well as a colourful and fascinating introduction to the picturesque and suggestive microcosm of Capri.

Here, in the Augustian age there was a sandy shore, the *Grande Marina* which the Romans used as a landing place for their ships and which afterwards became a port, situated in a more easternly location than the present infrastructure in harmony with *Punta Vivara*, from where one reached the imperial residence of **Palazzo a Mare**. The traces of this ancient maritime landing place, fortified and reinforced by Tiberius who wanted to facilitate communications between it and the fleet which was quartered in the roadstead of Misseno can still be seen today and give testimony of the important role of the island in the most splendid era of the Roman Empire, between the first century B.C. and the first century A.D.

Today Marina Grande is a beautiful riverside town which is set in a lovely natural position at the foot of the green saddle along which the romantic town of Capri stretches. The town of Marina Grande has merged with the above lying main town; in the small square which overlooks the port and which is usually swarming with tourists stand the characteristic houses of Capri, rendered typical by the terraces, by the balconies, by the open galleries and by the multicoloured facades of the town, brightened by the "Pompeian red" which is one of the most intense notes of colour along the whole Neapolitan coast.

The first sensations felt by the tourist, the first contact with this unique island, are of a fairytale nature: one's gaze, which is at first drawn to the picturesque port, to the boats and to the sequence of enchanting houses, is then directed to the green slopes which dominate Marina and which allow one to catch a glimpse of the first few houses of Capri, on the summit of the saddle. Amidst the steep terraced slopes, covered with an exuberant and blooming Mediterranean flora, or otherwise covered with vines, stand out the marvellous foilage of the maritime pines, whilst the white houses scenically set out in the shape of an amphitheatre on the background of the steep

Marina Grande: its boats, its colours, a Roman column situated on the harbour.

Boats in the enchanting background
of Marina Grande.

crags of calcareous rocks which all contribute to form a part of this wonderful Mediterranean crib.

Each end of the port of Marina Grande has two imposing wharfs at the end of the western wharf there is a *Coloumn* with a corinthian capital, placed on a high pedestal and this is proof of the important significance (even felt today) of the Roman presence on Capri. In the eastern part of the port a modern, well-equipped tourist dock is used by the sailors and by the beautiful boats which help to underline the tourist "enigma" and world-wide fame of this dream island.

However the most "vivid" aspect of Marina Grande is the large number of fishing boats, moored along the waters of the shore line or beached along the shore. Here,

in front of the houses (which were once used as ware-houses) the fishermen of the island carry out their work, either mending their multicoloured boats or repairing their nets while they wait for the most favourable moment to set sail.

During the tourist season, one can see, on the western wharf the coming and going of boats and hovercrafts which provide the connections between the mainland and the island, and numerous boats, motorboats and all types of craft set sail crowded with tourists to carry out the round trip of the island. The boat trip around the island, like the visits to the numerous **Grottoes** and to the **Faraglioni** can only be carried out when weather conditions, the sea and the tides permit.

The cable-railway which connects Capri to Marina Grande. It passes along the cultivated slopes and along the hills which seem to cling to the imposing rocks.

CABLECAR

The presence of this unique transport system is bound to be noted by the tourist. Although a modern road allows the taxis and public transport systems (during the season the use of private cars by the non-residents is strictly forbidden) to travel as far as the main town, thousands of tourists and travellers chose to take this lovely rack railway which goes on a direct route from Marina Grande to Capri.

The route of the railway goes along the fertile terraced slopes which descend from the saddleback along which the main town lies, right down as far as the riverside town below. It is a delightful experience to use this singular and rather old fashioned form of transport, which, however, is in harmony with the rough and wild nature of the island an aspect that is mirrored in the steep rocky peaks that one can see from the windows, and which dominate the characteristic houses dotted along the mountain slopes, with their terraces and arcades facing the horizon, set amongst the vines and crops which alternate with the lush evergreen scrub.

The panoramic look-out post.

On the following pages: the famous Piazzetta of Capri, a noted tourist place on the island.

CAPRI

This is the main town and the major centre of the island and stretches along the saddleback which lies between Mount St. Maria, Mount Tuoro and Mount Tiberius. Due to the spectacular beauty of its natural position (inserted in a geographical context of marvellous landscapes) Capri is considered to be one of the "pearls" of world tourism, the main goal of the tourists who visit the "minor islands", as well as being a place which is visited by tourists who come from all over the world.

The irresistible fascination of this extraordinary town is rendered above all by the salient traits of the towns and houses of Capri, which mirror the Mediterranean forms of architecture, such as the unending sequences of white houses which are all the more enchanting because of their terraces and loggias. A secondary characteristic element is the topographical order of the town, which is a picturesque labyrinth of streets and alleys which are often alternated or crossed by narrow lanes, surmounted by arches and arcades-clear proof of the ancient Medieval plan of the town.

The *piazza Umberto 1* is universally known as the "**Piazzetta**": it is the throbbing heart of the main town as well as being the main tourist attraction of the island. Once known as the "little theatre of the world" it is really the "drawing room" of Capri; at the tables of the cafès, which are shaded by multicoloured and characteristic umbrellas, the most important and prestigious people from the world of the cinema, fashion, literature, and politics and the composite world of buisness have sat.

It is an important meeting point and an obligatory stop for the crowds of tourists who come here throughout the whole year. The small piazza opens out on the site of where the first Greek colonies established the acropolis, between the V and the IV centuries B.C.. Imposing traces of the ancient tombs of Capri, built in the Greek period are still visible near the mountain cablecar station, inserted amongst the houses and the town perimetry which has a Medieval plan. The small piazza is dominated by the **Clocktower**, once the belltower of the ancient cathedral, and has a small cupola which has a decidedly eastern

Some charming views of the "Piazzetta", with the typical cafés. Opposite, the Church of Saint Stephen.

stamp, under which small arcades which house the bells open out. At one end of this charming centre lies the **Town Hall**, once the residence of the Bishop, which has a facade covered with plaques, whilst opposite this building stands the animated facade of the **Church of St. Stephen** which can be reached by a small flight of steps. Beyond the Clocktower, the piazza opens out onto the small loggia of *Belvedere*, characterized by a succession of white coloumns placed on high pedestals. From the parapet of the small loggia one can admire one of the most spectacular views of the whole island, which stretches out from the unmistakable profile of Ischia to the Flegrea region and the whole Neapolitan gulf, dominated by the menacing outline of Vesuvius. The view is particularly enchanting in the late evening when the numerous lights of Capri are seen against the dark profile of the mountains, softened by the twilight, and making an enchanting fairylike picture which is almost like a Christmas crib.

The cupola of St. Stephen, which has an almost oriental influence.

THE CHURCH OF ST. STEPHEN

This place of worship acts as a frame for one of the most characteristic views of the picturesque small piazza. The building which we see today is the result of a late 17th century project presided over by the architect Picchiatti and brought to completion by Marziale Desiderio of Amalfi who gave the typical forms of the architecture of Capri a decidedly Baroque characteristic. The exterior of the building (which stands on the site of a primitive cathedral, of which only the *Clocktower* remains) is characterized by its facade, enlivened by the curvilinear architecture upon which are inserted some tambours, these being surmounted by beautiful eastern-style cupolas. The building is dominated by a central dome, opened at the base by a series of arched windows. The facade, consisting of two orders, has a decidedly Baroque aspect, as can be seen by the curvilinear trend of the upper order, enriched by ornamental motifs. The upper order, vertically scanned by pilaster strips has two large niches containing statues. The most important artistic element that one can admire inside the church is the floor under the main altar: this is of a series of colourful pieces brought here from the *Villa Jovis*, the most celebrated of the many villas of Tiberius. In the *Chapel of the Rosary* some fragments of another Roman floor have been set out, which, in all probability was transfered from another Roman residence: the *Villa of Tragara*. Amongst the other works of artistic interest, the funeral monuments of the Arcucci should be noted. These were carried out by the Florentine sculptor Michelangelo Naccherino (16-17th century), and also a picture dating back to the XVIth century depicting the *Madonna with Child and Saints Michael and Anthony*. This painting is the object of particular devotion amongst the people of Capri, because legend has is that it played a part in a miracle which is thought to have taken place during the time of the pirate raids on the island.

PALAZZO CERIO

The bulding is situated at the extreme end of a piazza which bears the same name, near the Church of St. Stephen. The building which is reached by a flight of steps is characterized by an arcade on the ground floor; here there once stood a fortress which dated back to the Angevin period (XIVth century) and which later underwent radical changes and restructuring. Inside the building the *Ethnological Centre of Capri* can be found. Here one finds significant documentation relative to the sculptures and Neolithic ceramics, collections of fossils and interesting archiological finds discovered in the soil of Capri. A great amount of the material on show here was discovered by the doctor and naturalist Ignazio Cerio who was amongst the first to undertake excavation work at the beginning of this century.

THE MEDIEVAL DISTRICT

All around the famous Small Piazza and beyond the Church of St. Stephen, a complex maze of lanes and narrow alleys testify the presence of a medieval borough at Capri. This enchanting district makes up one of the most exhaustive pictures of the whole island, thanks to the buildings, to the setting out of the town and to the architectural techniques adopted during the Medieval period, offering at the same time a faithful reconstruction of town layout and structure which is common to Southern Italy and in particular to the Campana region.

The small houses which are almost superimposed on one another are separated, by small lanes, along which one can walk with difficulty, where the slopes alternate with the descents and which all join up in large open spaces where other roads meet, these latter lanes being characterized by flights of steps, by graceful arches which succeed one another or by long and dark covered lanes which are rendered all the more suggestive by shops and workshops.

Once again the dominant colour is the whitness of the house fronts, which are for the greater part built of calcareous stone and tufaceaos material. This uniformity is sometimes broken by the large patches of an intense azzure of the almost unreal sky of Capri, whilst the greennes of the vegetation seen in the hedges, in the bowers and in the lush gardens, rich in Mediterranean species and thriving examples of cactai here seems to come into its own.

Amongst the most important architectural buildings of the Medieval district we find the 17th century **Church of Salvatore**, built by Dionisio Lazzari, which, with the adjoining *Convent of the Tertiary*, forms a structural unity which is typical of the XVII th century. The picturesque small **Church of St. Anna** (XIIth century) looks out onto a small courtyard and in fact makes up a structural unity with the adjoining houses.

Evocative view of the Medieval part of Capri.

Via Vittorio Emanuele, with its boutiques, its craftshops and its hotels.

LARGE HOTELS

A stone's throw from the Piazzetta the Via Vittorio Emanuele stands one of the widest roads of the historical centre of Capri and it in fact divides the Medieval quarter from the area of the large hotels. The road ends right in front of the Grand Hotel Quisisana where the Via Camerelle and the Via F. Serena begin. Along these two streets, which lead one to the *Belvedere of Tragara* and the *Gardens of Augustus* respectively, can be found other luxury hotels. These streets are characterized by the extremely pretty buildings and by the graceful elegance of the architectural lines which, even tough they echo the forms of building common to all Mediterranean islands, are not without their own majesty and grandeur.

In the last ten years Capri's importance as a tourist spot has increased enourmously, not only during the tourist season but also during the winter months and notably during the Christmas holidays and New Year when it is possible to take part in the folkloristic displays, enlivened by the unique sound of the putipu. These holidays and

visits to the island, along with the Easter holidays and the so-called "weekend" tourism all form to contribute an important economic incentive for the island, and render the streets of the town centre if not overcrowded at least nearly always full of people.

Together with the large hotels one can also find along these streets, as with many other in the town, characteristic shops selling handicrafts and refined and exclusive boutiques where it is possible to buy the best products on the market, along with the classic characteristic souvenirs of Capri; ceramics, majolica, coral, artisan products made of cord. The epicurean only has the embarrasment of choosing what he would like to eat at the shops and the ice-cream parlours which produce excellent (and usually homemade) ice-cream.

Amongst the curiosities which this part of the island holds it should be remembered that in 1905, during excavation work carried out on the foundations of the Grand Hotel Quisisana, important archeological and paleantological objects were found.

THE GARDENS OF AUGUSTUS

This green park, shaded by the pine trees and brightened up by the presence of many species of flowers, palm trees and other forest trees is a "breathing space" situauted not far from the town centre. Its pleasant position which dominates the underlying complex of the *Certosa of St. James*, where the Via Krupp winds steeply up from the Marina Piccola, makes it an ideal resting place for tourists and travellers. From a nearby look out post one can look out onto the marine horizon, a view which embraces one of the most important panoramic sights of the coast of Capri with its incredible variety of steep rocky inlets and which is marked by cliffs near which the imposing and fascinating outline of the *Faraglioni* rises up out of the waters.

Two views of the luxuriant vegetation of the Gardens of Augustus.

Via Krupp and the Charterhouse of St. James as seen from above.

VIA KRUPP

The panoramic road, which can only be undertaken on foot because of its narrow dimensions is one of the most noted attractions of this pleasant Mediterranean "gem". It was built at the beginning of this century by the famous German industrialist whose name has been given to the road itself. Picturesquely cut into the rocks which characterize the rocky cliffs of the southern coast of Capri, it goes from the *Gardens of Augustus* to *Marina Piccola*. Those who love Capri will not fail to miss the spectacular transparency of the turquoise waters of the limpid depths where, here and there, one can catch a glimpse of the submerged rocks. The cliffs that fall sheer down to the sea can be seen in the most enchanting of views, and are covered with the Mediterranean scrub, by the agaves, by the Indian figs and by the everpresent cactai. Further down a Saracean **Tower** commemorates the ancient fights for the possession of the island.

THE CHARTERHOUSE OF ST. JAMES

This building, seen from above the scenic *Belvedere of the Cannon* reveals features of the monumental magnificence, rendered even more peculiar by the Medival architectural forms of Capri, and has examples of obvious 17th century influence. The rough and undulating profile of the buildings, with their ample display of curved lines and cupolettes gives the complex the characteristics of a decidedly eastern and vaguely Arabian construction even if the real architectural quality of the Charterhouse is anything but eastern in style.

It is an important testimony of the Dark Ages of the Medieval period, surviving the raids and invasions of the pirates and it is almost hidden in the lowland, immerged in the green and lush vegetation which rises up almost like a wall along the slopes and the surrounding reliefs. The characteristics of the landscape of this spot are difficult to forget: from the thick interlacing of the Mediterranean

The Little Cloister of the Charterhouse of St. James.

scrub alternated by maritime pines, agaves, Indian figs and cypresses, stand the residential homes of Capri with their balconies, their wide terraces and their beautiful loggias, whilst here and there patches of the intense azzure of the swimming pools of the luxury hotels can be seen.

It seems certain that the place where the modern Charterhouse stands today was one of the few places neglected by the Romans, during the period of major changes which the island underwent, and was neglected because of the numerous constructions, imperial villas and residences for the ruling classes which were being built at this time. It is quite probable that the people who built the Charterhouse wanted to take advantage of the steep, impervious and rocky coast which formed a natural defence wall and was therefore easily defended.

The founding of the Charterhouse was sponsored, in the second of the XIVth century by Giacomo Arcucci, secretary to Giovanna I, Queen of Naples and the Counts of Altamura and Minervino. The suggestive forms of the archaic buiding do not do justice to their architects and designers, who are unknown. It soon grew in splendour and economic power, but the Charterhouse was then subjected to desecration and devastation caused by the pirate Dragut (second half of the XVIth century) however it was then restored, enlarged and furnished with a better look-

out system so as to anticipate the constant risk represented by the Corsairs who swarmed the waters of the Tyrrhene Sea. Suppressed by Guiseppe Bonaparte in the first years of the XIXth century, mutilated by the crumbling of the 16th century defense tower, it then went into an irreversible decline and was then subsequently used as penal baths, an institution and a place of military confinement.

It was only in more, recent times that the Charterhouse was restored to its ancient splendour, being used as a centre where congresses on tourism are held and where exhibitions of ancient and contemporary art can be seen. The most ancient parts of the monastic complex can be found around the *Little Cloisters*, graced by elegant arches which stand on small columns, by cross vaults and brightened up by the oleanders which surround the central well-curb, dominated by the Baroque cusp of the so-called *Clocktower*. This part of the charterhouse, where we can find the *Church* and the *Refectory* imitates the trend of the Cistercian monastic architecture whilst the *Great Cloister*, the product of a 16th century addition, denotes structural affinities with that of the Neapolitan charterhouse of San Martino. The external buildings are the *Store-Rooms*, the Cellars and the *Residence of the Prior*.

The Church, which has only one nave maintains an extremely bare and linear aspect. Worthy of note is the beautiful doorway, which is Gothic (ogival) in style, in whose lunette is a frescoe of the XIVth century depicting "*The Virgin and Child with Saint Brunone and Saint James with Queen Giovanna and Count Arcucci*. The apse, illuminated by a three mullioned window surrmounted by quadrilobes, holds fragments of frescoesand stucco ornaments dating from the XVIIth century.

In the buildings near the Church the **Museum of the Charterhouse** can be seen, which contains, amonst other things, sculptures which have been severly corroded by the salt water of the Blue Grottoe. Such findings would seem to back the hypothesis that the most famous of the grottoes of Capri was, in Roman times a sort of magnificent temple consecrated to the nymphs and was part of the Imperial Villa of Damecuta. Amongst the other works of art worthy of mention are a series of paintings dating from the XVIIth to the XIXth centuries and also the sinister canvases of the German artist Kurt Willhelm Diefenback. The paintings of this artist, who lived on the island and died here in 1913 are characterized by a dark, gloomy pessimism with evident reference to the sepulchral theme and to the concept of death.

The Museum of the Charterhouse: two sculptures found in the Blue Grotto and the frescoes of the Church of the Charterhouse.

On the following pages: enchanting views of the southern coast of Capri and the Faraglioni.

FARAGLIONI

Emerging from the unfathonable depths of an extraordinary and intensely blue sea, these enigmatic colossi of rocks have always constituted the most famous and popular image of Capri throughout the world. Even though, in other places, other rocks of a similar form and dimension are called by the same name, those of Capri are the *Faraglioni* "par excellence".

Situated in front of the south-eastern coast of the island, they were formed by the age-old erosion of the waters which broke off "walls" of rock from the central body of the island and also formed cracks, cavities grottoes and beautiful natural arches, moreover the relentless action of the erosion which took place can be seen all along the coast of Capri, especially in this region.

Subdivided into *Faraglioni of the Earth*, the *Middle*

Faraglioni and the *Outer Faraglioni* they reach a height of respectively 111,81 and 105 mts. Nearby, in front of the so-called Porto di Tragara, stands the "Scoglio del Monacone". A favourite spot with photographers, they are easily reached by boat and make up one of the obligatory stops of the journey around the island. Their waters, limpid and profound, are a paradise for all those interested in nature and underwater diving; on the outer Faraglione lives the rare *Lacerta coerulea faraglionensis*.

The imposing majesty of the Faraglioni of Capri never cease to amaze the visitor.

Marvellous examples of rocks and natural arches of the "magical" waters around the Faraglioni.

A view of the Natural Arch.

THE NATURAL ARCH

This strange natural phenomenon, together with the Faraglioni and the Grotto of Matermania is one of the most famous tourist spots on this part of the island. One gains access to the Arch by a flight of steps which is cut off by a path frequented by tourists. This itinerary describes a sort of circular trip around Mount Tuoro leading out from the centre of Capri to the houses on the outskirts of Matermania, along via Camerelle, via Tragara and via Matermania. This excursion which permits the tourist to admire in all its wildest beauty the marvellous scenario of the Faraglioni, the evocative southern coast of the island with its picturesque coves, the projections, the inlets and the parts of the island which stretch out into the turquoise marine waters can be highly recommended.

The Natural Arch is the visible remainder of an ancient Karst cavity, destroyed by the landslides which broke up parts of the island of the island. It was moulded by the erosive action of the exogenous agents. Its pleasant position, in the midst of a thick pine forest which reveals glimpses of the sea constitutes one of the most attractive motifs of the whole island.

The steep flight of steps which leads to the Grotto of Matermania; on the right, the Faraglioni and the port of Tragara.

GROTTO OF MATERMANIA

Following the scenic itinerary which broadens out in front of the natural beauty of the Faraglioni, one goes upwards to the Cove of the Fig Tree, at a height where, stretched out along the narrow Punta di Massullo, the unmistakeable profile of the *Casa Rossa* stands out. This villa was once owned by the Tuscan writer Curzio Malaparte.

A little further ahead a fork in the road leads to the Grotto of Matromania. Also known as the *Grotto of Matermania* it is a natural cavity where the ancient orgiastic customs were practised. These rites were part of the worshipping of the *Mater Magna*, and were also frequently carried out on the Sorrento peninsula at the height of the Imperial Age and were similar th those of Cybele. In its present state the grotto shows the elaborative work which was carried out by the Romans, who reinforced the natural vaults with walls and decorated the grotto with mosaics and stucco work of which only scarse and fragmentory traces remain. The latest archeological findings would suggest that the grotto was used as a temple (where nymphs were worshipped) where the small quantities of water which oozed out of the rocky vaults collected.

Two views of Marina Piccola, with the bathing resorts and the Rock of the Sirens.

MARINA PICCOLA

This evocative town is one of the most well equipped and fashionably famous seaside resorts of Capri, as well as being a small landing place for the nautical enthusiasts and tourists who have the possibility of mooring their crafts here, along a naturally protected and sheltered coastline. Marina Piccola is symmetrical to Marina Grande since it constitutes the main landing place and the principal port of call for navigational services.

Marina Piccola has its own particular character, more cosy, graceful and attractive; alongside its delightful coves. Between the 1950-1960's the reputation of Capri as a tourist Mecca flourished. This "boom" was thanks to the presence on the island of the most famous names of the film-world, the cultural world and that of show buisness.

However there are numerous indications that the place was populated as far back as the most remote ages. Along the rocky spurs which are outlined along the eastern side of Mount Solaro, one finds the *Grotto of the Ferns* which dominates the underlying Marina and which represents one of the most important prehistoric sites of the whole island. Archeological excavations have brought to light a numerous quantity of domestic objects as well as the remains of funeral objects and primitive ceramic objects. This grotto, populated as far back as the Neolithic Bronze Age, acted as an important lookout post along the southern coast. In the Imperial Age, the Romans used it to reinforce the characteristics of the natural landing place; some building work done on the ancient Roman port are still visible today near the so-called *Rock of the Sirens*.

Today the enchanting vision of Marina Piccola can be en-

A view of Marina Piccola.

joyed by those who reach it by means of either the road which bears the same name, or by the evocative Via Krupp. The delightful ''Rock of the Sirens'' (or ''of the Mule'') forms a natural barrier between the *Marina di Mulo* which stretches out in a westerly direction up to the Point bearing the same name, and the *Marina di Pennauto* which stretches to the east up to the powerful outline of the Faraglione. In addition to the numerous tourist and seaside infrastructures Marina Piccola has typical restaurants and fashionable ''haunts'' such as the famous ''Canzone del Mare'' (''Song of the Sea'') which during the ''roaring'' years of the Cinema became one of the meeting points for artists of world renown.

Marina Piccola is one of the main starting points from where one sets out (either with one's own personal craft or with the one of the numerous public transport boats) along the journey around the island. This trip allows one to enjoy the considerable scenic beauties of the island, the fascinating outline of its rocky coasts, marked in several places by marvellous natural cavities and by steep and impending cliffs. The boat trip allows one to pass near the Faraglioni, - immense and solitary rocky giants-or even to penetrate in their natural arches through which one can pass.

A panoramic view of Marina di Pennauto with the Grotto of Castiglione; the Saracean Tower.

On page 36: some enchanting views of the so-called "Red Grotto" (Grotta Rossa), known in ancient times as the "Grotto Rufolo". It takes its present name from the mosses which cover the rocky cliff walls.

On page 37: three views of the Green Grotto. Once known as the Grotto dell'Orefice, it owes its present name to the emerald tones that, at certain times of the day, depending on the light, colour its waters.

A view of the Castle of Castiglione.

THE CASTLE OF CASTIGLIONE

The climb up to the panoramic spot of Castiglione is without doubt amongst the most worthwhile if only for the enjoyment of the spectacular scenic views which can be seen in the direction of the Faraglione and towards the towns of Capri, which emerge from the Mediterranean scrub, wonderfully set round in the shape of an amphitheatre along the slopes of the natural saddle which separates Marina Grande from Marina Piccola.

This pleasant excursion allows one to observe in all their entirety, the unadulterated buildings of marked Medieval influence which make up one of the most characteristic and important examples of the ancient urban arrangements of the historical centre of Capri. The Castle of Castiglione, as one sees it today has the characteristics bestowed on it by restruction work and by restoration work which was only finished in quite recent times. The powerful embattled ramparts and the huge square reinforcement towers, which are also surmounted by a crown of merlons, stand on the summit of a rocky peak. The side of the building which faces the sea seems to fall in steep crags and cliffs of bare rock in which the gigantic Grotto

of Castiglione can be seen, down towards the sea, whilst on the side facing the Charterhouse of St. James is covered by a thick verdant undergrowth, from which some magnificent and typical residences seem to peep out at one.

The Castle of Castiglione was originally a Medieval structure, built on the site of an ancient Greek acropolis. During the numerous pirate raids the Castle was an important defensive rampart for the population of Capri (even though most of the population used to take shelter in the *Grotto of Castiglione.* This grotto, which was once a prehistoric seat since the Neolithic era, was used by the Romans as a temple, connected to an *Imperial Villa* above the grotto. At the Villa one can make out the remains of walls of *opus reticulatum*.

This magnificent villa, which stands on the northern slopes of Castiglione, was discovered at the end of the XVIIIth century by the Austrian archeologist Norbert Hadrawa. It seems that in numerous rooms, later hidden by a disasterous attempt to cover up the villa, a large amount of interesting and valuable exhibits were found, such as mosaic and marble floors, frescoes and stucco decorations which were unfortunately lost after the plundering of the Villa by Hadrawa himself.

VILLA JOVIS

The majestic remains of a magnificent Roman villa dating back to the Imperial Age stand above the plateau which culminates in the so-called Mount Tiberius (335 m) The Villa which bears the name of the most important of the Olympian divinities is the most representative of a consistent number of villas built on Capri during the Augustan-Tiberian eras.

A written tradition, quoted by Tacitus would attribute Augustus' successor with the building of twelve imperial residences all dedicated to the Consenting Gods (Jupiter, Apollo, Neptune, Mars, Vulcan, Mercury, Juno, Minerva, Venus, Vesta, Ceres and Diana).

The itinerary which takes one to the important archeological site is amongst the most trodden and frequented by tourists, not only for the exceptional attraction which this extraordinary testimony of the Roman presence on Capri holds, but also for the halo of mystery, and at the same time, the great and dissolute power which surrounds the figure of Tiberius and the myth surrounding the man which is echoed in the anecdotes heard on the island even today. From the centre of Capri, first taking the via Sopramonte and then taking the via Tiberius which leads into the via Moneta one can easily reach the spot where the Villa stands. This route runs along a gentle but continuous slope which is characterized by narrow streets flanked by beautiful gardens, parks and residences and rural orchards; here and there one gets marvellous glimpses of the scenery towards Capri and its roofs, brightened by the typical architecture and immersed in the dazzling brightness of the white houses. In the most favourable season the oleanders are in bloom, the leaves of the Indian figs and the characteristic outline of the agaves enliven the walks of the tourists and the visitors who can breathe in the unmistakable perfume of Capri,

The main entrance to Villa Jovis.

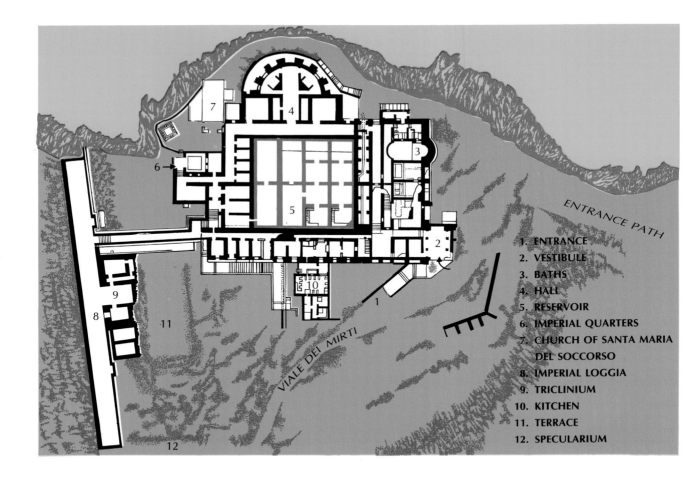

1. ENTRANCE
2. VESTIBULE
3. BATHS
4. HALL
5. RESERVOIR
6. IMPERIAL QUARTERS
7. CHURCH OF SANTA MARIA
   DEL SOCCORSO
8. IMPERIAL LOGGIA
9. TRICLINIUM
10. KITCHEN
11. TERRACE
12. SPECULARIUM

perhaps stopping a minute to contemplate the astonishing qualities of a place which has been so generous to Man. A little before the ruins of the Villa Jovis, on the right, stand the broken remains of another Roman tower. Here, there once stood a *Lighthouse Tower*, an ancient light system used for signaling by either fire or smoke. During Tiberius' stay on Capri, this structure was particularly important as it permitted the Emperor to have daily communication with the mainland, by means of a beam situated on the facing Punta Campanella, at the extremity of the Sorrento peninsular. In such a way Tiberius decided the destiny of the Empire during the last years of his tormented reign.

From the same tower contact was also kept with the lighthouse of Capo Miseno, in whose roadstead the imperial fleet rode at anchor. Due to a strange coincidence the Lighthouse Tower crumbled during sismic tremors a little while before the death of Tiberius; it was later restored and used as a lighthouse to defend the ships of the island up until the XVIIth century.

There have been many discussions about the figure of Tiberius, discussions which more often than not linger over details of his supposed vices and perversions rather than on his virtues and qualities as a ruler of the boundless Empire of Rome. We should not forget however, that

many of the anecdotes, which refer to the successor of Augustus, whether they are true or not, are, the result of stories told by narrators who were clearly biased and definitely hostile towards Tiberius. It would therefore be appropriate to reflect, separating fiction from fact, on the terrible punishments which he inflicted on families and servants whom he felt were unloyal, on the capital punishments carried out by throwing his enemies into a bottomless abyss (known today as *Tiberius' Leap*) as well as the slaughtering of young men and women which took place in the Blue Grotto after the licentious erotic games in which both sexes took part. Concerning these facts Axel Munthe writes ("*The History of Villa St. Michael*" Publishers: Garzanti, 1940) "As to the sinister traditions of Tiberius, handed down through the ages by the *Annals* of Tacito the "detractor of humanity" as Napoleon called him, I said to Lord Dufferin that History had never made such a big mistake as when it condemned this great Emperor to such infamy only on the testimony of his greatest accusors. Tacito is a splendid writer but his *Annals* are historical fiction, not History... That Tacito himself didn't believe the stories about the orgies on Capri is clear from his own narritive, since he doesn't play down to even one degree his general conception of Tiberius as a great Emperor and as a great man "of ad-

mirable character and much respected" to use his own
words. Even his much less intelligent follower, Svetonio
recounts the most filthy stories, making the observations
that it is hardly admissable that they should be told let
alone believed... Tiberius was 68 when he retired to Capri
with a reputation for having led a strict and moral life
still intact, and not even damaged by his worst enemies.
The possible diagnosis of senile dementia can be exclud-
ed, because all the historians maintain that the old man
was in full possession of his faculties and was physically
fit up until his death at the age of 79. Moreover the streak
of madness which ran through Giuliano's family was ab-
sent in that of Claudio. His life on the island was that of
a solitary old man, of a tired ruler of an ungrateful
world, a gloomy idealist with a shattered and bitter heart
(today one could call him a hypercondiriac), but a man
with a magnificent intellect and rare spirit still having
faith in humanity. It is little wonder that he had no trust
in his contemporaries and that he hated them because
almost all the men and women in whom he had put his
trust had betrayed him...".

The principle nucleus of Villa Jovis or *Palazzo di Tiberio*
stands on the summit of the most extreme eastern slope
of Capri, in a scenario of inexpressible beauty. Above the
ruins rises the small *Church of St. Maria del Soccorso*
built on the site of a medieval place of worship dedicated
to *St. Christopher* and *St. Leonard*. Nearby is a statue of
The Virgin and Child, from where one can look out over
the whole island, taking in the endless horizon which
sweeps from the distant Ischia to the Neapolitan gulf
dominated by the characteristic profile of Vesuvius, as
far as the nearby Punta Campanella and the wide gulf of
Salerno.

The main part of the ancient imperial construction
revolves around the mangnifent complex of the *water
tanks* which were used to provide water for the entire
complex of the Villa collecting the rain water in spacious
impluvia. All around are to be found the various interiors
which have been discovered and which have a total surface area of over 7000 square metres; it is believed
however that the Villa Jovis with its various outlying
buildings covered an even vaster area. Particularly interesting are the remains of the wall which sometimes
show elements of *opus reticulatum* and sometimes elements of *opus incertum*, whilst often the floors have a
herring-bone pattern (*opus spicatum*). At the side of the
water tanks the actual *imperial residence* is situated,
which leads to the so-called *imperial loggia*. The latter
which has a triclinium and exedrae was the spot favoured
by Tiberius for his walks.

Another conspicuous portion of the villa is the *baths*
which show the classical division of the Roman thermal
constructions: *Apodyterium* (changing room), *Frigidari-
um, Tepidarium*, and *Calidarium*. A complex heating

Tiberius' Leap: now that the cruelty of the Roman
emperor has been forgotten, only the natural beauty
of the rocks which drop down into an incredibly
clear sea, remain; the Lighthouse Tower.

system (hypocaust) was used to heat the waters. Next to the church of St. Maria di Soccorso, right at the edge of the rocky slopes which fall sheer to the sea are the remains of what has mistakenly been called a *Temple* (where nymphs were worshipped). In reality this was a hemicircular room used as a meeting place where the imperial chancellery held audience.

In a position set apart from the complex of imperial buildings, one can see the ruins of what must have been the kitchens and store houses of the Villa. A little further away from the main part of the Villa, near the steep slope which descends to Marina Grande can be seen the ruins of massive walls and vaulted constructions. In all probability these are the ruins of a *Specularium* (Observatory) which was also used to communicate with the lighthouses on the coast of the Campana region.

On the road leading to Villa Jovis, a scenic lay-by allows one to contemplate the serene beauty of the island. In the background Mount Solaro dominates the houses of Capri, whilst below right, stands the town of Marina Grande, which faces the picturesque port.

THE BATHS OF TIBERIUS

The conspicuous remains emerging from the turquoise transparency of the marine waters which run along the front of the northern coast of the island, in harmony with the so-called *Houses of the Palace on the Sea* constitute a visible testimony of the marine quarters of a magnificent imperial Villa of the Augustean age. The traces of the Baths of Tiberius which can be visited today consist of a sloping wall which leans against a slope rich in vegetation but liable to slide down; of a small area destined to be used a dwelling place; of a temple with adjoining exedra, used for fish production and some service structures for a small landing stage suitably defended by walls against the disintegrating action of the breakers.

Many modifications and transformations carried out over the centuries and the complete absence of a large central nucleus do not allow one to immediately perceive the exact location of the original *Palatium* (palace) of Augustus. We know for certain that the emperor had a soft spot for the place which is today occupied by the Houses of the Palace on the Sea and that the villa which stood here was certainly more sober and less imposing than the sumptuous proportions of the villa that his successor, Tiberius, raised on the brink of the steep precipices which face the Sorrento peninsular.

The *Villa of the Palace on the Sea* is the only one of the numerous imperial villas which is situated close to the sea and which occupies a marittime position as opposed to the traditional elevated positions favoured by the Roman architects who worked on Capri.

Fragmentary archeological findings which have come to light have shown us the characteristics of a country residence, with wide spaces set apart for gardens and for the emperor's walks. Today the Tiberian foundations which are known as the Baths of Tiberius are the only parts which have withstood the onslaught of time and the thoughtless plundering by the Austrian Hadrawa in the 18th century, stripping the Villa of the Palace on the Sea of many architetonic furnishings and artistic decorations. Afterwards, during the 19th century the area was used as a military base by the French and the English who further contributed to the ruining of this important archeological site which today is populated by private residences, hotels and rural dwellings.

A panoramic view of the Baths of Tiberius as seen from the small Loggia of the Villa St. Michael; one can clearly make out the transparency of the waters.

The magic Blue Grotto.

THE BLUE GROTTO

The Blue Grotto is counted as being one of the major tourist attractions of Capri. This Karst cavity, together with the equally famous Faraglioni has contributed in spreading the enigma of this island all over the world. The most traditional and evocative way of carrying out this excursion, which shouldn't be missed during the course of a visit to Capri, is to take one of the tourist boats or motorboats from the Marina Grande. The visit to the Blue Grotto, which can only be undertaken if weather and sea conditions permit should take place, if at all possible, in the morning so that one can enjoy the play of light which reflects the marvellous chromatic effects of underscribable fascination and evocativeness. It would be very wise to avoid the guided tours with the inevitable overcrowding mass of tourists during certain periods of the year (National Holidays, long week-ends and the high season) as there will bound to be long queues at the embarkation points and outside the entrance to the Blue Grotto, as well as a marked decline in the evocative effect obtained inside the grotto, due to the presence of too many overcrowded boats of noisy tourists.

The Blue Grotto which was a well-known and favourite place with the Romans, fell into oblivion and it became shrouded in fear, mystery and superstition blown out of all proportion by the inhabitants of the island who were convinced that the grotto was a meeting place for witches and that horrifying monsters lived there. It seems quite probable however that an increase of the bradysismic phenomenon almost closed off the access to the grotto. It was already the subject of much discussion with both scholars and map-readers as far back as the XVIIth century and was then rediscovered in 1826 by two daring and bold German travellers, the writer A. Kopisch and the painter E. Fries. Since those days a constant and endless stream of visitors and tourists have visited the place as well as a great number of Italian and foreign literary scholars, who have drawn inspiration from the place.

Outside the grotto, whilst waiting patiently to pass through the narrow entrance way, it is possible to observe the remains of the *Villa of Gràdola*. This building, also known as the *Villa of Gradelle* is a Roman construction of secondary importance if one compares it with other, more conspicuous traces of the Imperial era. For a while it lent its name to the grotto which lies below if, before this became known by the name which extols its predominant colours. However the particular predominance that the more well-known imperial residence of the *Villa of Damecuta* assumed in this would support the hypothesis that the Blue Grotto was used by the Romans as a marine temple (where nymphs were worshipped). Such a hypothesis is strengthened by the presence of building work of the Roman period found inside the grotto and by the discovery of sculptures submerged by the bradysismic actions and corroded by the sea water. Today these statues can be seen inside the Charterhouse Museum of St. James.

The atmosphere of magic seduction inside the Blue Grotto is obtained by the sky-blue reflections of the beams of light which penetrate through the narrow access hole, whilst the extraordinary cobalt-blue transparencies are caused by the light diffused under the mirror of the waters and which filters through an underwater opening. This opening was probably a primeval cavity submerged during ancient tectonic upheavals.

THE PHOENICIAN FLIGHT OF STEPS

In spite of its name which refers explicitly to the Phoenicians — who definetely lived on the island and used it as a commercial landing place along their routes in the lower Tyrrhene Sea — this impervious rocky flight of steps is one of the few proven surviving traces of the Greck colonization of the island.

The walk which consists of over 800 steps cut into the bare rock climbs up the north-eastern buttresses of Mount Solaro and has for centuries been the only means of communication between Anacapri, the rest of the island and more importantly with the landing wharfs of Marina Grande.

The achievement, during the last century, of a means of communication between the two main centres of Capri and Anacapri has granted the Phoenician Flight of Steps the role of a tourist route, still trodden by fishermen and tourists who would like to discover the landscape marvels of the island along this ancient rocky itinerary which, however tiring, allows one to enjoy a more direct and natural relationship with the unparalleled enviroment of Capri.

The entrance to the Blue Grotto and the Scala Fenicia (Phoenician Flight of Steps).

A panoramic view of Anacapri and the small loggia of Villa St. Michael with the ancient Sphinx.

ANACAPRI

Splendidly set out along the gentle slopes which descend from the steep sides of Mount Solaro, the second most important centre on Capri is set out like on oil stain on the vast thickly-cultivated plateau, in a context of shimmering Mediteranean beauty. It was an elevated settlement during the Greek presence on the island and was a favourite haunt of the patricial Roman families who built numerous villas here; loved and frequented by Tiberius who spent many long periods at the imperial villa of Damecuta, it was also chosen by the illustrious Swedish humanist and medic Axel Munthe as a home. Munthe, in his "*The History of St. Michael*" has wonderfully captivated and handed down to the following generations, the image of this oneeric and fairytale-like enchanted island. Even today, in spite of transformations undergone due to the huge numbers of tourists, Anacapri has managed to retain its characteristics as a typically elevated centre on a Mediteranean island. The white houses, with their decidedly "Caprese" architectural lines, are set out in

their bright splendour (given to them by the whitewashed fronts, by the airy and luminoius terraces, by the often curvilinear volutes of the roofs of the buildings). All around, a lush vegetation betrayed by the gardens, by the orchards and by the bowers can be seen, whilst the neighbouring districts are marked by the presence of myrtle, juniper, lentisk, broom and by various other species, alternating with the maritime pine and the Aleppo pine.
Anacapri is an ideal holiday village and a renowned health resort which enjoys the benefits of an extraordinary mild and healthy climate. As a starting point for interesting naturalistic excursions and also history trips, it is clustered around the beautiful **Parish Church of St. Sophia**. This was built during Medieval times and is brightened up by the central cupola, by the small minor cupolas and by the majestic *Clocktower*. The elegant Baroque facade (XVIIIth century) in two orders is vertically divided by pilaster strips.

The entrance of Villa St. Michael.

VILLA ST. MICHAEL

The architectonically eclectic and extremely heterogeneous construction is situated in the town of Capodimonte, on the edge of a steep slope which falls sheer to the underlying Baths of Tiberius. Included within a fantastic landscape context which offers aspects of touching pleasantness, it stands out thanks to the brightness of its composite architectonic attitude amongst the arrogant greenness of the lush Mediterranean vegetation and the cobalt-blue patches of the marine waters below. On the site where Axel Munthe started to build the villa, from 1896 stood a rural dwelling which even today, even if it has been transformed, makes up the central nucleus of the buildings. During excavation work, a great number of the remains of the buildings dating back to the Imperial times were discovered; even today the conspicuous remains of the walls of *opus reticulatum* would support the theory that this site was the ancient seat of the *Villa of Capodimonte*, one of the 12 imperial residences of Augustean-Tiberiean foundation.

However, let us quickly run through (almost as in a film) the salient moments of the construction of the Villa St. Michael just as Munthe himself described in *"The History of St. Michael"* (Published by Garzanti, 1940)... "Finally we arrive at the top of the 777 steps and pass under a vault with the huge iron hinges of the first drawbridge, still a part of the rock. We were at Anacapri. The whole gulf of Naples was at our feet, surrounded by Ischia, Procida, Posillipo, decorated by pines, the scintallating white lines of Naples, Vesuvius with its pinkish cloud of smoke, the plains of Sorrento protected by Mount Sant'Angelo and the faraway Appennines covered in snow. Immediately, above our heads, almost like an eagle's nest placed at the top of the rugged rocks, were the ruins of a small chapel. Its vaulted ceiling had caved in, but rising up from its crumbling walls were large blocks of stone, which formed a strange and open-worked symmetrical pattern. "The work of Tiberius" explained Maria, the old woman.

"What's the name of the old chapel?" I asked politely.

"St. Michael". "St. Michael, St. Michael!" my heart repeated. In the vineyard underneath the chapel, an old man was digging new deep furrows for the young vines... After five long summers of unending work, from dawn to dusk, St. Michael was more or less finished, but there was still a lot of work to be done on the garden. A new terrace was to be built behind the house, another loggia was to be built above the two small Roman rooms which we discovered in the autumn... Looking at it once again, St. Michael seems more beautiful to me now than before. The house was small, there were very few rooms, but there were the loggias, the terraces and the bowers all around the villa, where one could look at the sun, the sea and the clouds-the soul needs more room to breathe than the body. Very few pieces of furniture in the rooms, but the few pices that were there couldn't be bought for just money".

Today, the Villa which has been left (through his will) to the Swedish state, is presided over by the well-merited *Foundation of St. Michael* which takes care of the indisputable maintenance work. In the summer season, Swedish scholars and humanists stay here, whilst a series of artistic, literary and cultural workshops are held after the expressed whishes of Axel Munthe: a complete integration of the cultural links between Sweden and Italy.

The entrance hall into which one passes through a beautiful doorway surrmounted by a semicircular mosaic frieze with a golden background and decorated with marble ornaments, has a mosaic floor depicting the Pompeii motif of *Cave canem*, a sculpted fragment of a Roman sarcophagus and a tombstone with epigraphs.

The dining-room is also decorated with an ornamental floor which has a copy of a mosaic of Pompeii and allegorical symbols with Bolognese furnishings in the Renaissance style; also to be seen are the collection of Swedish pewter objects dating from the XVIIIth century.

The entrance hall forms part of an inner enclosed garden which brings to mind the ancient Roman residences. Also worthy of mention is the extremely valuable Roman well-crib which dates back to the Republican period and which has many delightful external bassreliefs. Some bronze heads/busts are copies of original Greek-Roman works, whilst the walls are decorated with ancient fragments of clay and marbleand a series of funeral epigraphs.

The bedroom which can be reached by the stairs and the loggia, has a strange iron bedstead in the Sicilian style of the XVth century, furniture belonging to the Florentine Rinascimento, bronze sculptures and a marble baserelief dating from the imperial period depicting *"Apollo playing the lyre"*.

AXEL MUNTHE

Born in Oskarshamm, in Sweden on the 31st of October 1857, he undertook his initial studies in Sweden and then attended University courses in France and took his degree in Medicine in Paris, at the early age of 23. After having worked as a doctor in the French capital he moved to Rome in 1890 and became a highly admired and much sought after doctor amongst the upper classes. Called to the Court of Stockholm in 1903, he spent long periods of his on Capri where he built the magnificent residence of St. Michael and it was here that he wrote his immortal masterpiece. During the last years of his life he was the guest of the rulers of Sweden and Stockholm. He died suddenly in the Ducal Palace on the 11th of February 1949. A man, doctor, humanist of indiscutable qualities, he threw himself with extraordinary altruism into the work of helping the needy, and in enviromental matters anticipated the most recent ecological developments.

In the *French drawing room*, the original edition of the "*History of St. Michael*" is on view together with numerous translations (done by Munthe) whereas on one wall the motto of Axel Munthe is painted ("To dare, to Wish, to Know and to keep silent").

The study, enhanced by a beautiful mosaic floor of marble, which was probably brought from Rome, holds many valuable and antique objects such as the *Head of a Youth* executed in terracota, noteable Greek works (dating from the IVth century B.C.) and a *Head of Medusa* which Munthe himself found in the marine depths of the Baths of Tiberius.

The adjacent *Venetian Drawing Room*, characterized by the Rococo Venetian furnishings is separated from the study by a beautiful marble coloumn, sustained by a elaborate capital.

The so-called *Loggia delle Sculture* opens out onto the delightful view of the bowers: the most important work of art is a marble bust depicting *Tiberius* or his descendant *Germanicus*. Amongst the other statues which are worth mentioning are a Roman reproduction of an original Greek statue dating back to the IVth century, B.C. of *Ulysses*. Numerous works of marble are to be seen and reproductions in sculpture which are quite well-known. In the middle of the loggia one finds an exquisite mosaic table, sustained by graceful spiral columns, also decorated by mosaic interlacings.

This work is attributed to the Cosmati, Roman marble workers, who carried out marble work as far back as the 12th century.

The *small bower* which culminates in a scenic absidal lookout post from where one can admire an enchanting view over the Neapolitan gulf, over the peninsular of Sorrento and over most of the island. In the surrounding districts obvious traces of the imperial Roman villa are evident.

The white *Chapel* dedicated to the archangel of the same name gives the title to the entire complex of St. Michael. It is situated on the ruins of a building dating back to the X century. On the side of the entrance hall is a funeral sculpture dating back to the Roman period and depicts the *Virgin and Child*. The interior houses a Rinascimental sculpture in wood representing *St. Michael* and a baptesimal font from the XIV century. Nearby the chapel, on a wall facing an extremely pleasant view is placed an Egyptian *Sphinx* in red granite, which dates back to the 11th century B.C.

Along the evocative *Avenue of the Cypress trees*, along which Munthe himself planted frutices taken from the garden of the Villa D'Este near Rome one can observe the bassreliefs of the tomb of Lucio Careio (first century B.C.), finally arriving at the atrium of the *kitchen*, where valuable ceramic vases from Faenza, dating back to the 18th century and used for pharmaceutical purposes can be seen.

A view of the Castle of Barbarossa.

THE CASTLE OF BARBAROSSA

The imposing turreted ruins of the Castle of Barbarossa appear in all their glory and turn one's gaze to beyond the scenic terraces of the Villa St. Michael. Due to its spectacular and impregnable position on the summit of a steep rocky crag this castle has been throughout the centuries an eagle's nest from where one could look out onto the endless green horizons and towards the coast of the region of Campana.

Some architectonic details such as the small chapel with apses which can still be made out within the main bulk of the buildings, support the hypothesis that this ancient castle, at least originally, formed part of a fortified structure built by the Byzantium race. The castle's name recalls the pirate raids carried out by Barbarossa who in 1535 overcame its defences, carrying out the worst pillages that the island ever suffered.

Behind the nickname of Barbarossa is hidden the real identity of Khair-ad-Din admiral and Turkish pirate born in Mitilene, who lived between the 15th and the 16th centuries. The famous Corsair who together with his brothers attacked the Aegian and north African coasts, finally establishing a small kingdom in Algiers which was the starting point for the pirate raids through the whole Mediterranean basin. After having conquered Tunisia (1533) he was given command of the Ottoman fleet by the Turkish sovereign Solimano. Solimano often blocked the fleet of Charles Vth as well as those of Genoa and Venice obtaining a position of superiority over the Christian fleet on the waters, culminating in the Battle of Lepanto (1571).

The Church of St. Michael at Anacapri: the white façade and a view of the interior.

The beautiful majolica pavement in the interior.

THE CHURCH OF ST. MICHAEL

This building stands out due to its Baroque facade in two orders which holds elements of considerable architectonic interest and has an undulating trend, rendered by the little arch above the main archway and by the coloumns of the ground floor. The upper portion of the facade is scanned by pilaster strips in the vertical sense, culminating in further small decorations in the form of long pyramids, whilst at the centre of the "crown" of the building stands a triangular structure. The interior, with its central hexagonal plan is considered to be one of the most marvellous architectonic and decorative masterpieces of the whole Campania region. This place of worship, was completed in 1719, based on a plan of the architect, painter and sculptor, Antonio Vaccaro, born in Naples and who lived between the XVII and the XVIIIth centuries.

The masterpiece of this church is the incredible majolica floor which the Abruzzese artist Leonardo Chiaiese carried out, probably under the auspices of Vaccaro and which depicts magnificently some allegorical biblical tales such as the *Earthly Paradise* and the *Expulsion form the Garden of Adam and Eve.*

From Anacapri one can reach the summit of Mount Solaro by means of a fast and comfortable cable-car.

An ancient Medieval cistern.

CABLECAR AND MOUNT SOLARO

The highest mountain summit along the relief of Capri (589 mts) can be reached on foot and starts off from Anacapri, crossing the cultivated slopes of the mountain and crossing the lush Mediterranean vegetation. For the laziest of travellers, a cablecar takes one directly from Anacapri to the summit from which one can make out some ruins of ancient fortified structures, built by the English.

From the scenic look-out post one can look out over the enchanting views of the Neapolitan gulf towards Ischia, dominated by the characteristic outline of Epomeo, towards the bridging islands, towards Naples laid out at the feet of Vesuvius and beyond the Sorrento peninsular as far as the Apennine mountains. Below lies Capri, whitened by the slopes of the saddle which precipitates into the sea with its rocky crags, whilst from the cobalt blue of its waters rises the gigantic and enigmatic outline of the group of rocks known as the Faraglione.

The not too distant hermitage of *St. Maria a Cetrella* merits a visit. The delightful 14th century architecture recalls the forms of the typical Caprese architecture and stands on the edge of the steep precipice which faces the Marina Piccola. The story which says that the the building is based on an the site of an ancient Greek temple consecrated to the worshipping of Venus and Citerea seems to have no actual proof.

The Look-out Tower dominates the steep and rugged precipice.

THE WATCHTOWER

The characteristic cylindrical outline of this stone tower stands at the limit of the rocky crags which face the Punta Carena. This fortified structure would also seem to have an important strategic role throughout the last century when it constituted one of the main defense structures of the apparatus used to guard the plains of Anacapri. Even today the tourist has the opportunity to visit the ruins which represent the indelible historic reminder of this part of the island. The remains of ancient fortresses, of castles, of towers and of look-out posts can be seen along the vast plateau which as a border, has only the eastern slopes of Mount Solario.

The excursion on foot can be highly recommended as far as the *Belvedere of the Migliara*; from this exceptional panoramic point it is possible to admire the wild profile of the coast of Capri, which in this part of the island is rendered particularly evocative by the scenic presence of the rocks of *Marmolata*, which rise up in the manner of fantastic Dolomite rocks.

THE TOWER OF MATERITA

What is commonly called the tower of Materita is, in fact, one of the most beautiful residences on Capri. The building, entirely crowned with merlons and surmounted by a beautiful tower is softened on both sides by elegant bifores. Above, the circle of merlons is sustained by an interlacing of overhanging brackets. The tranquil solitude of this place, surrounded by an olive grove and vines in the midst of a small cypress wood and lush vegetation inspired Axel Munthe, who here, finished his book "*The History of St. Michael*".

In his masterpiece, speaking of Materita, he wrote (op. cit. Publishers: Garzanti, 1940) "I have finally accepted my destiny. I am too old to fight with a God. I have retired and have come to my fortress, to the old towers where I intend to resist for the last time. Dante was still alive when the friars began work on the Torre di Materita which is half monastery, half fortress as solid as the rock on which it stands. "There is no greater sorrow than to remember happy times in times of sadness". How many times has this bitter phrase echoed around the walls since I've come here! But after all, was the Florentine right? Is it true that there is no greater sorrow that to remember past happiness in times of sorrow? I don't think so. It is with joy and not with sorrow that my thoughts go back to St. Michael, where the happiest years of my life were spent. But it is true that I no longer like to go there: I feel as if I am intruding on sacred ground, a sacred past that will never return, when the world was young and the sun was my friend.

It is bliss to wander along in the soft light, under the olives of Materita. It is lovely to sit and meditate about the old tower and it is the one and only thing which I can do... The tower looks eastwards, to where the sun sets. Soon the sun will sink into the sea, then twilight will come and then the night.

It has been a lovely day...".

The tower which was originally built in the XVth century and constituted an integral part of the coastal defense structure against the threat of the pirate raids was bought and restored by the Swedish writer who loved it and used it as a place for reflection and meditation. Even today the interiors hold a large number of interesting works of art, memorabilia and souvenirs connected with the stay of Axel Munthe on Capri.

The Tower of Materita stands out from the thick Mediterranean vegetation. The ruins of other fortified buildings are to be found along the western coast.

Ruins in "opus reticulatum" of the Villa of Damecuta.

A view of the Tower of Damecuta. ▶

VILLA DI DAMECUTA

The flat plains of Damecuta stretch out along the north-western portion of the vast plateau of Anacapri. In the Imperial Roman era this area was chosen by the architects of the capital who built a great number of villas and residences here. In virtue of its excellent geographical position, and its pleasant exposition to the rays of the sun and to the sea breezes the area around Damecuta soon became a residential area for the patriarchial Roman families. Amongst the many buildings, several of which were in fact farms, those of *Aiano, Montivello, Tiberino* and *Vitareto* stand out.

Along the margin of this idyllic scenario on the plateau of Anacapri near the Medieval Tower of Damecuta lies the vast archeological area which has rendered traces of one of the most imposing and magnificent Roman villas

of the Imperial period: the Villa Damecuta. The origins of the place name seem to be lost in the times of the Greek colonization of the island; the hypothesis that Damecuta seems to be derived from *Domus Augusti* seems to have no foundation in fact.

The complex visissitudes of this great imperial building, haunted by the figure of Tiberius and his myth, obscure and worrying but at the same time luminous and fascinating were brought to light at the beginning of the second half of the 1930's. At that time the generosity of Axel Munthe, the owner of the place, allowed the archeologists to procede with the work of salvaging the remains of the ancient building.

It also seems certain that this villa was the first of the Imperial villas of the island to be abandoned; seriously lesioned by the fall of materials of a piroclastic nature from the eruptions of Vesuvius, during the destructive episodes which wiped out Pompeii, Ecolano and Stabia (79 B.C.) almost completely submerged by the volcanic material, it fell into decline. Afterwards it underwent frequent pillaging and plundering throughout the ages and also underwent destruction during its transformation into a military base for the Bourbons and for the English who stripped it of its considerable architectural patrimony. This building, as others on the island must have had a large number of ornaments, pictures, stucco work sculptures, mosaic or marble floors.

Today it offers a place for contemplation for visitors especially the work in *opus reticulatum*, whilst in other places can be found the more simple examples of *opus incertum*. In particular the *Loggia* stands out, facing the steep panoramic brink which falls sheer down to the underlying marine abysses. This was the favourite place of the Emperor for his walks, and is enriched by numerous exedrae. A little below lies the embattled **Tower of Damecuta** a strong fortress in stone blocks, built during the XIIth century so as to guard over the moves of the Corsair boats lies the imperial *Domus*. Here in what must have been the bedroom of the Emperor an acephaleos bust has been found depicting *Narcissus* (nude) a clear example of the refined tastes of Tiberius and his lascivious leanings. It seems certain that the Villa had a flight of steps which led down to the sea, near the modern day Punta di Gradola and near the entrance to the Blue Grotto, where the remains of another Roman villa are clearly visible.

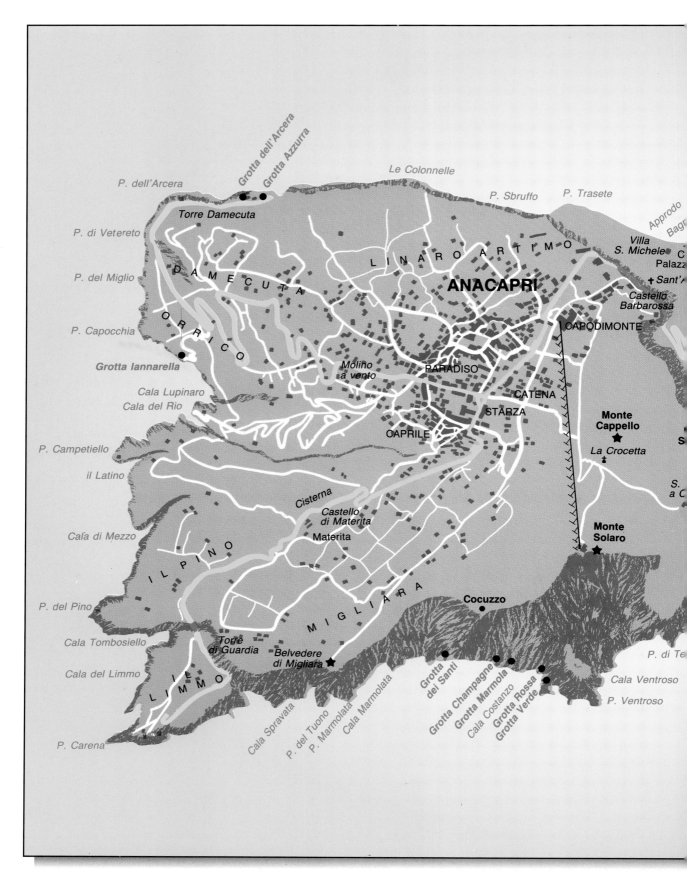

P. del Capo

La Fossa

Scoglio Longa
di basso

Grotta di Ricotta

Scoglio La Longa
di Mezzogiorno

P. Fucile

**Monte
Tiberio**

Grotta del Bove Marino

P. Caterola

Palazzo
di Tiberio
(Villa Iovis
Rov.)

S. Maria
del Soccorso

Marina
di Caterola

**Grotta
di Tiberio**

P. del
Monaco

Torre
del Faro

io Ricciuto

P. Vivara

Ufficio
Turistico

MARINA
GRANDE

CESINA

La Chiavica

P. della
Chiavica

MONETA

Funicolare

**Grotta Meravigliosa
Grotta Bianca**

CAPRI

Faraglione di Matermània

MONGIARDINO

Arco
Naturale

Grotta dei Preti

MATERMÀNIA

Grotta Matermània
Cala di Matermània
a basso Furno

Giardini
di Augusto

Certosa
di S. Giacomo

Grotta Massullo

P. di Massullo

**Grotte
Castiglione**

Castiglione
Belvedere
Cannone

**Monte
Tuoro**

Cala del Fico

Via Krupp

MARINA
PICCOLA

Marina di
Pennauto

Grotta
dell'Arsenale

Grotta oscura

Belvedere
di Tragara

Tragara

ina
ulo

Grotta dei Coralli

Scoglio delle
Sirene o di Mulo

Grotta Albergo
dei marinai

Grotta di Forca

Porto di
Tragara

Scoglio del Monacone

Arco di Stella

Approdo

Faraglione di terra

P. di Tragara

Faraglione di mezzo

Faraglione di fuori

IL CAPO

CONTENTS

© Copyright by CASA EDITRICE BONECHI
Via Cairoli 18b - 50131 Firenze, Italia
Tel. +39 055576841 - Fax +39 0555000766 -
E-mail: bonechi@bonechi.it - Internet: www.bonechi.it

Printed in Italy by Centro Stampa Editoriale Bonechi.

Texts: Giuliano Valdes, Editing Studio, Pisa.

The photographs are property of the Casa Editrice Bonechi Archives and were taken by Paolo Giambone. Photo Amendola: page 46. Photos Barone: pages 3, 42/43. Photos Farella: pages 14, 16, 21, 22. Photo Tripodi: page 5. Photos Realy Easy Star/Spagone: pages 6, 17.

* * *